# ENTERTAINMENT WARRIOR

## GOING GREEN

by **Claudia Martin**

Consultant: David Hawksett, BSc

**BEARPORT**
PUBLISHING

Minneapolis, Minnesota

Credits: cover top, © Tanyastock/Shutterstock; cover bottom, © Nyo09/Shutterstock; 1, © Elwynn/
Shutterstock; 4b, © Vchal/Shutterstock; 4–5b, © Monkey Business Images/Shutterstock; 5t,
© Sunsinger/Shutterstock; 6t, © Nataliia Budianska/Shutterstock; 6b, © Veja/Shutterstock; 7,
© Pochatenko/Shutterstock; 8–9t, © Heiko Kiera/Shutterstock; 8–9b, © Dzmitry Palubiatka/
Shutterstock; 10–11b, © SmLyubov/Shutterstock; 11t, © Photosync/Shutterstock; 12, © Ulrich Mueller/
Shutterstock; 13, © Young Swee Ming/Shutterstock; 14, © Iofoto/Shutterstock; 15, © Radu Bercan/
Shutterstock; 16t, © Iofoto/Shutterstock; 16–17b, © Andrius Kaziliunas/Shutterstock; 18, © StunningArt/
Shutterstock; 19, © Ken Wolter/Shutterstock; 20, © Darren Baker/Shutterstock; 21, © Sutipond
Somnam/Shutterstock; 22, © AL Robinson/Shutterstock; 23, © Creatikon Studio/Shutterstock; 24,
© Anghi/Shutterstock; 25, © Elwynn/Shutterstock; 26–27b, © Tatiana Popova/Shutterstock; 27t, ©
Aleksandra Suzi/Shutterstock.

Editor: Sarah Eason
Proofreader: Jennifer Sanderson
Designer: Paul Myerscough
Illustrator: Jessica Moon
Picture Researcher: Rachel Blount

*Library of Congress Cataloging-in-Publication Data is available at www.loc.gov or upon request from the
publisher.*

ISBN: 978-1-64747-696-0 (hardcover)
ISBN: 978-1-64747-703-5 (paperback)
ISBN: 978-1-64747-710-3 (ebook)

For more information, write to Bearport Publishing, 5357 Penn Avenue South, Minneapolis, MN 55419.
Printed in the United States of America.

# CONTENTS

The Battle to Save Earth!......... 4

Swap Your Toys........................... 8

Get Wise to Packaging ............. 12

Save Your Books ....................... 16

Keep Your Consoles ................... 20

Beware Batteries....................... 24

Eco-Activity: Make Your Own Slimy Toy ..................... 28

Glossary.................................................................. 30

Read More ............................................................... 31

Learn More Online.................................................... 31

Index...................................................................... 32

# THE BATTLE TO SAVE EARTH!

Do you prefer to play board games, flip through the pages of a book, or game on a screen? Whichever way you have fun, you are one of billions of people using **products** for entertainment—and they're not so fun when they pile up as waste. But you can battle this waste without sacrificing the fun by being a wise waste warrior!

## The Three Problems with Waste

**Heaps of Garbage**  We toss more than half our trash into **landfills**. But when waste breaks down in landfills, it can harm our environment. **Plastic** can leak harmful things into the soil and air. Waste in landfills lets off methane gas as it breaks down. On top of that, the waste just sits there—stored for a future generation to deal with. That is why waste warriors avoid creating waste!

We have created landfills to deal with our huge amounts of waste.

**Wasted Resources** Electronic game consoles and robotic toys contain metals, such as copper, silver, and aluminum, which must be **mined** from the ground. Earth has a limited amount of these **natural resources**. Not being responsible with these metal toys wastes our planet's resources.

**Polluted Planet** Toys and games are made all over the world. When these products are transported to kids in other places, **fuel** is burned to power the engines of planes, boats, trucks, and trains. Burning **fossil fuels**, such as gasoline, releases **carbon dioxide** and other **greenhouse gases** into the air. These gases trap the sun's heat around Earth and raise the temperature of the air and ocean. The increase in temperature is causing **global climate change**.

The process of mining for metals harms our planet because it creates **pollution**.

Plastic toys and games can take up to 1,000 years to break down when they are thrown away.

# The Six Rs

How can you become a waste warrior without being bored? There are six simple ways that waste warriors can battle waste. Don't worry if it takes a while to get the hang of it. Just keeping one plastic brick out of a landfill is a step in the right direction.

**Refuse** If you have a choice, say no thanks to any free toys you are offered at the doctor's or dentist's office.

**Reduce** Instead of shopping for all the latest collectibles, try to cut back on extra toys by only picking things that won't fade with the fads.

**Reuse** Before throwing out old toys, ask yourself if a younger sibling or neighbor could have fun with them.

**Repair** If possible, fix broken toys and electronics rather than buying new ones.

**Recycle** Recycle all the plastic, paper, glass, and metal toy packaging and products that you can.

**Rot** Some kinds of fabrics can rot. See if your old stuffed toys can go in the **compost** bin rather than the trash.

Reducing screen time also reduces waste. It means you will use less electricity to power and charge your devices.

Once you have outgrown toys, box them up and donate them to younger kids.

Electronic games are often made of plastics and metals that do not easily break down. Consider fixing broken electronics whenever possible.

# SWAP YOUR TOYS

Take a look at the toys and games in your home. From beads to balls, most toys contain plastic. Although many plastics can be **recycled**, most plastic toys can't.

Plastic toys and games aren't accepted by curbside recycling programs because they usually contain a mixture of different plastics and metals. Before these toys can be recycled, the different types of materials that they are made of need to be separated, which is too time-consuming for recycling centers. The result is that plastic toys usually end up in landfills, where they stay for up to 1,000 years. Over time, they may leak harmful chemicals such as phthalates into the soil and water.

Machines or people sort waste at recycling centers. If a piece of waste is made up of many different materials and can't be sorted, it will probably end up in a landfill.

The phthalates from thrown-away plastic may make their way into the ocean. Phthalates have even been found in the eggs of sea turtles.

What a **Waste!**

Around 90 percent of toys purchased in the United States are made of plastic or contain plastic parts.

What can a waste warrior do with piles of plastic playthings? First, play! Get good use out of the plastic toys you already have. Then you can extend the life of your well-loved toys further by donating them or organizing a toy swap with friends or other kids in your neighborhood. Next, think carefully before you get new toys. Ask your family and friends to avoid giving you plastic toys as gifts.

## Warriors Can Try:

Here are some tips for organizing a toy swap.

- Ask friends and family if they have toys that they no longer use.
- With an adult's help, agree on a time and location for the toy swap.
- Spread the word about the swap.
- Ask everyone to bring toys that are in good condition, without missing pieces.
- Meet up and trade toys you don't use for ones that are new to you.
- Donate any leftover toys.

Someone will play with your supercool toy cars even if you're done with them.

Wooden toys are **biodegradable** when the fun is over.

# GET WISE TO PACKAGING

Many toys are packaged to keep them clean and secure while they are transported and sold. Cardboard boxes, wire ties, plastic containers, and packing foams wrap new toys and create a world of waste. Wasteful toy packaging is anything but playful.

Packaging is often made of materials that are difficult to recycle. Flexible plastic containers, often called clamshells, are an example of this problem packaging. Clamshells are usually made from a common plastic called **PET**, but most curbside recycling programs cannot recycle them. The plastic molded for clamshells needs to be melted at a higher temperature than other plastic products, such as drink bottles. As a result, most clamshells have to be tossed in the trash.

Creating toy packaging causes pollution—packaging factories pump harmful gases into the environment.

# What a Waste!

In 2017, people in the United States threw away more than 14 million tons (12.7 million MT) of plastic packaging.

Clamshell containers are used all over the world—and they create a world of waste.

A waste warrior can battle packaging waste by taking a few simple steps. The best way to reduce packaging waste is to buy fewer toys. That doesn't mean you can't play—just buy wisely, choosing items that will be played with for a long time. If you want to take it a step further, pick toys that have packaging using only one easily recycled material, such as cardboard. Other good choices are packaging made from recycled plastics or from **bioplastics**, which come from plant materials that will biodegrade on a compost pile.

# Warriors Can Try:

Take these steps when recycling toy packaging.

- Remove the windows of plastic film that are stuck to many cardboard boxes; the cardboard can be recycled but the plastic has to go in the trash.

- Flatten cardboard boxes so they can be transported easily to the recycling center.

- Save the wire ties that connect toys to packaging. They are not recyclable but they can be reused!

Flattened cardboard boxes take up less space in your recycling bin.

The best type of
packaging is no packaging!
Look for toys without any
packaging at all.

# SAVE YOUR BOOKS

More than three billion books are bought every year in the United States. Most of these books are printed on paper rather than downloaded as ebooks. While paper can be recycled, hardcover books usually can't be, which means a waste warrior needs to find a smart solution for old books!

Hardcover books cannot be recycled because the pages are glued together at the spine, which means glue goes into the mix when paper is broken down in a recycling plant. A whole batch of recycled paper can be spoiled by glue. And if paper biodegrades in a landfill, the biodegrading **bacteria** produce a gas called methane. If the methane is not carefully captured at the landfill, methane can worsen **smog**. It is also a powerful greenhouse gas that increases global warming.

Donating books to a library or charity will keep them safely out of a landfill. It's a no-brainer!

# What a Waste!

Landfills in the United States release more methane than in any other country. They account for more than 16 percent of the world's 882 million T (800 million MT) of **emissions**.

The smog surrounding this city was caused by gases, including methane.

A waste warrior can find plenty of ways to pass along used books. Start by offering your old reads to siblings and friends. To make it more fun, write a short review of each book so friends can decide if it's the kind of book they enjoy. Group books by type, such as science fiction, adventure, or nonfiction. Then, friends can stick with their usual choices—or try something new!

## Warriors Can Try:

You can donate your used books to others. Here are some places that might take old books.

- Thrift stores
- Schools
- Libraries
- Doctors' offices
- Children's hospitals

Try setting up a book exchange with a friend—it's a great way to recycle your books.

A great way to make use of old books is to set up a free library.

LittleFreeLibrary.org®
Take a Book · Return a Book
Charter # 37298
A Nonprofit Organization

# KEEP YOUR CONSOLES

Don't toss your tech! Game consoles, electronic toys, computers, and tablets that are reaching the end of their useful life are all types of electronic waste, often called e-waste. Around 80 percent of e-waste is tossed in the trash. E-waste is one of the world's worst waste problems because it can be dangerous, not just to the environment but to the workers who **process** it.

Some parts of e-waste can be recycled. However, e-waste also contains very harmful materials that can damage our organs and bones. More than half of the e-waste collected in the United States for recycling is transported to other countries. There, sometimes recycling methods endanger workers and release hazardous materials into the air, soil, and water.

It's fun to play electronic games, but they are not so fun for Earth.

Workers who recycle our e-waste are sometimes exposed to harmful materials.

# What a Waste!

Every year, the world throws away around 55 million T (50 million MT) of e-waste.

The first thing you can do as an e-waste warrior is to go on gaming with the same device. You don't need that new model to have fun! When you're really finished with your device, try to pass it on to a friend, thrift store, or youth center. If it's broken beyond repair or you can't find a home for it, ask an adult to help you find a recycling company that handles e-waste safely.

## Warriors Can Try:

If you don't think the maker of your favorite electronic game is doing enough to tackle e-waste, try writing them a letter.

- Explain why e-waste is a global issue.
- Offer suggestions for how they could reduce e-waste, including bringing out fewer new models, making products longer-lasting, and setting up a responsible recycling program.
- Ask an adult for help with checking and sending.

Hey, Waste Warrior—don't throw out your e-waste! Instead, seek out stores that will buy or exchange your games and devices.

ENTERTAINMEN
EXCHANGE
WEBUY.COM

PHONES   GAMING   ELECTRONICS   DVD

BUY   SELL   DONATE     WE ♥ RECYCLING

E-waste piles up in recycling centers like this one. Tell your family and friends about the problem, and ask them to find waste warrior solutions to e-waste, too.

# BEWARE BATTERIES

Batteries power many things, including drones, cameras, computers, and even cars. But batteries can give only a certain amount of energy before they stop working. Which means, sooner or later, you'll probably have a waste problem on your hands. Unfortunately, batteries are one of the trickiest forms of waste to safely dispose of.

Depending on the type, batteries may contain cadmium, mercury, lead, lithium, or zinc. These are all **toxic** materials that will damage the body if they are breathed in or swallowed. If batteries are thrown in the trash, they could end up in a landfill, where they could leak poisonous materials into the soil, rivers, and lakes.

Old batteries create a huge waste problem.

# What a Waste!

People in the United States buy nearly three billion batteries every year, with about 179,000 T (162,000 MT) of them eventually ending up in landfills.

A lot of toys, such as this drone, are powered by batteries. When the batteries run out, they need to be replaced—and the old ones need to be disposed of.

A great way to reduce battery waste is to buy rechargeable batteries. They cost more than **disposable** batteries but can be recharged hundreds of times before needing to be recycled. That's a win for a waste warrior! When disposable or rechargeable batteries no longer work, ask an adult to help find a battery recycling program. Properly recycled batteries are safely separated into different materials and made into new products—including more batteries!

# Warriors Can Try:

Here are some tips for extending the life of your batteries, so you can use fewer.

- Remember to switch off electronics after using them.

- If you won't be using a toy for a while, ask an adult to take out the batteries and store them in a safe place.

- If a gadget has a low-power setting, remember to use it.

BATTERIES
ONLY

BATT
ON

Batteries recycled in
used battery bins will
not end up in a landfill.

The best batteries can be
recharged. They may be
more expensive to buy,
but they will help you
save money—and the
planet—in the long run.

## Eco-Activity
# Make Your Own Slimy Toy

Do you want a new toy without the waste? Unlike store-bought slimes, oobleck doesn't contain plastics or glitter, which can pollute rivers and streams. It doesn't come in wasteful packaging or use up the charge in a battery. Make your own toy that's simple, squishable, and super fun! Have a blast with homemade oobleck!

## You will need:
- 1 cup of water
- A small bowl
- Natural food coloring (optional)
- 2 cups of cornstarch
- A large bowl
- A metal spoon
- An airtight container for storage

1 Pour your water into the small bowl. Then, add a few drops of food coloring if desired.

2 Add your cornstarch to a large bowl.

3 Pour about half your water into the cornstarch. Mix with a spoon until combined.

**4** Add more water, a little bit at a time, until the oobleck is gooey enough for you to squeeze it into a ball.

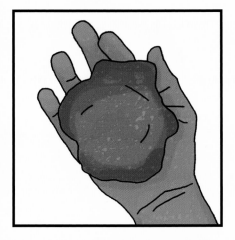

**5** Now you have made what scientists call a non-Newtonian fluid, which flows like a liquid when it is left alone but behaves like a solid when it is under pressure. Experiment with your toy.

**6** Your oobleck can be stored for a while in an airtight container, but you may need to add a little more water when you play with it again.

**7** When it's time to get rid of your oobleck, don't pour it down the sink or toilet because it could cause a blockage. But your oobleck is completely biodegradable, so you could toss it in a compost bin.

# Glossary

**bacteria** tiny, very simple living things

**biodegradable** can be broken down

**bioplastics** plastics made from plants and other natural materials, rather than from oil

**carbon dioxide** an invisible gas in the air that is released when fossil fuels are burned

**compost** rotted plants and food that can be used to feed soil

**disposable** intended to be used and then thrown away

**emissions** released gas, pollution, or energy

**fossil fuels** fuels made from the remains of animals and plants that lived long ago

**fuel** a material that can be burned to make heat or power machines

**global climate change** the change of Earth's climate and weather patterns, including the warming of Earth's air and oceans, due to human activities

**greenhouse gases** gases, including carbon dioxide and methane, that trap the sun's heat around Earth

**landfills** pits where waste is dumped and then covered by soil

**mined** dug out from underground

**natural resources** useful materials found in nature, such as trees, water, metals, and oil

**PET** a plastic often used to make packaging

**plastic** a machine-made material, usually made from oil, that can be shaped when soft, then sets to be hard or flexible

**pollution** any harmful material that is put into the ground, air, or water

**process** a series of steps taken to make or achieve something

**products** things that are made then offered for sale

**recycled** collected, sorted, and treated waste turned into materials that can be used again

**smog** a fog of air pollution

**toxic** poisonous

# Read More

**Berg, Shannon**. *E-Waste in Guiyu, China (21st Century Disasters)*. Lake Elmo, MN: North Star Editions, 2020.

**Latham, Donna**. *Garbage: Follow the Path of Your Trash (Build it Yourself)*. White River Junction, VT: Nomad Press, 2019.

**Wheeler, Adrienne**. *Waste Disposal (Earth's Environment in Danger)*. New York: Rosen Publishing Group, 2018.

**Yanish, Brian**. *Scrapkins: Junk Re-Thunk*. New York: Henry Holt, 2016.

# Learn More Online

1. Go to **www.factsurfer.com**
2. Enter "**Entertainment Warrior**" into the search box.
3. Click on the cover of this book to see a list of websites.

# Index

**batteries** 24–28
**books** 4, 16–19

**compost** 6, 14, 29
**consoles** 5, 20

**donate** 6, 10, 17–18

**e-waste** 20–23

**fossil fuels** 5

**games** 4–5, 7–8, 20, 22
**global climate change** 5
**greenhouse gases** 5, 16

**landfills** 4, 6, 8, 16–17,
    24–25, 27

**natural resources** 5

**packaging waste** 12, 14, 24, 28
**plastic** 4–10, 12–14, 28
**pollution** 5, 28

**recycled** 6, 8, 12, 14, 16, 18, 20–23,
    26–27
**reduce** 6, 14, 22, 26
**reuse** 6, 14
**rot** 6

**toys** 5–6, 8–12, 14–15, 20, 25–26,
    28
**transported** 5, 12, 14, 20